About the Author

Mala grew up in Hyderabad, India where she learnt to love Hyderabadi cuisine. She now lives in London with her husband, two grown-up children and a dachshund.

Hyderabad

A Memory of Taste

For Sonia,

With love from,

Mala.

by Mala Gole

With illustrations by
Elizabeth Adams

Cover Illustration: The Charminar, Hyderabad

First Edition Published in 2020 by

Mala Gole
14 Oakford Road
London NW5 1AH
United Kingdom

Hyderabad
A Memory of Taste

Book Design by
RIM Creation / Raphael Iruzun Martins

Printed and Bound in the UK by Leiston Press

ISBN 978-1-911311-76-8

Contents

Thanks go to my friend, Liz, for making my vision a reality with her incredible artwork. Raphael Iruzun Martins helped with the design, for which I am grateful. My mother checked my memory, and my mother-in-law dotted the i's and crossed the t's, both of whom I thank for their input. My father urged me on in my journey. My husband, Vivek, and children, Arjun and Lulu, remain my food fans and critics, and I have needed them to practise on for the past 27 years! But, most of all, I thank Sharifabee for introducing my taste buds to this special cuisine, and to whom I dedicate this book.

Introduction

I first learned to appreciate Hyderabadi cuisine after my father moved there on work. Arriving at Nampally Railway Station in 1971, after a three-day 1,445 km journey, we were taken to the grand Greenlands Guest House. This was to be our home for the next few weeks, while looking for a more permanent home. I can still remember the taste of the first mouthful of chicken biryani I had there.

My parents found a lovely house that we moved into in Banjara Hills. This is where we spent all our years in Hyderabad and had the privilege of employing the best cook in the world, Sharifabee. She loved my brother and me like her own children and cooked each meal with passion. She took great pride in feeding us well, introducing us to what became our great love, Hyderabadi cuisine. Today, my mother and I take the same pride in cooking for our family and friends.

We had a great mix of friends in Hyderabad, without any thought given to religious differences or places of origin. We celebrated Diwali, Eid and Christmas with equal joy with friends and neighbours. This made growing up there a very special experience as we developed a taste for different cultures, learnt the distinct Hyderabadi dialect and sampled a wide variety of cuisine. In the early days when my brother and I were growing up, we would cycle at speed up and down the steep roads of Banjara Hills and fearlessly climb the huge rocks there. We loved every day at school and our early teenage years were joyful. Throughout this period, Hyderabad was a very special home to us. Memories of weekends spent at the Sailing Club and Sunday lunches at the Secunderabad Club will live on forever, as will the aroma of fresh mackerel and crabs transferred directly from the sea to the pan during our holidays on the beach in Chirala.

The Charminar, built by the Qutb Shahi rulers in 1591 to mark the end of a plague in the city, is named for the four ornate fluted minarets at its corners. This combined monument and mosque, one of the most recognisable landmarks in India, is a prime example of Indo-Islamic architecture. The four clocks were added in 1889.

In order to highlight the intricate design of this building, a minimalist approach was taken. The sky, trees and street have a very soft watercolour wash. The crowds, cars and buses were not included. The pen and ink was softened in places with a watercolour wash.

- Elizabeth Adams

Mohamed Quli Qutb Shah established Hyderabad in 1591 and became its first ruler. Since then, despite changing hands several times, Hyderabad has been known for its Persian architecture and rich culture. It has also been a major pearl and diamond trading centre.

The *Koh-i-Noor* and the blue Hope diamonds came from mines nearby. Today Hyderabad is a modern city with manufacturing, pharmaceutical research, financial and information technology industries, while maintaining its old charm of traditional bazaars, courteous people and delicious food.

Hyderabadi cuisine has had many influences, both native and foreign. Banquets were popular during the reign of the Nizams of Hyderabad and remain so to this day at weddings and festivals. The chefs, known as Khansamas, were highly regarded by the aristocracy and the cuisine was, and continues to be, thought of as an art form.

This great cuisine has evolved over centuries from medieval times, and reached the modern period through the work of skilled chefs serving the nobility of the Deccan, most importantly in Hyderabad, the capital of the richest kingdom in the area. Here was a centre of innovation, led by the royal *Khansamas*, that eventually gave form to modern Hyderabadi cuisine. These recipes were the closely guarded trade secrets of the *Khansamas*, and originally only passed on directly to their heirs by example and training. The recipes included here are based on the ones dear Sharifabee had learnt from her family which she cooked so lovingly for us.

The use of traditional pots and pans with copper bases, and high quality ingredients has always been essential, all of which add to the taste and aroma of the food being cooked. Slow cooking on low heat is the key, done patiently, *ithmenaan se*, and with love.

I tend to cook from my 'memory of taste' rather than from a fixed recipe and sometimes look to my mother for guidance to confirm my instincts. The Hyderabadi recipes in this book are some of my favourites, written down as I remember them. You will find most of the recipes in this book cooked in a Hyderabadi home. My love for the City of Pearls remains alive through my enjoyment of its royal cuisine, often lined with warq.

The recipes in this book serve 4.

The government-owned Greenlands Guest House is to go back to being a VIP guest house, after being used as administrative offices by the new state of Telangana for several years. Luckily, as a notified heritage structure, it has escaped being razed and replaced by a modern multi-storey building.

The building is outlined with pen and a very pale wash was applied. There is just a hint of brickwork shown in pen on the facade so as to keep the building simple. The foliage and garden is also toned down from the original photo with a light wash of green to depict the grass. The trees are more defined as they provide a contrast with the pale building.

- Elizabeth Adams

Breakfast

A day begins better with a Hyderabadi breakfast
of Khageena, Parathas and a cup of Elaichi Chai

Khageena

Indian Scrambled Eggs

Ingredients

8 medium eggs
1 onion, finely sliced
2 tsp ginger & garlic paste
1/4 tsp turmeric
1/4 tsp salt, or to taste

2 fresh green chillies
2 tbsp fresh coriander leaves & stem
2 tbsp vegetable oil

Method

1. Break the eggs in a bowl and mix them gently with a fork and set aside.
2. Heat the oil in a large frying pan then turn the heat down before adding the sliced onions. Fry the onions for 5-7 minutes until soft and opaque but not brown.
3. Add the ginger & garlic paste, turmeric and salt and mix well and cook for a further 5 minutes.
4. Cut the green chillies as finely as you can, de-seed them if you prefer it less hot, and add them to the onions.
5. Add the eggs to the pan, and stir very gently.
6. Chop and add the fresh coriander. Stir in gently.
7. Cover and cook on low heat for 7-10 minutes, stirring gently half way, until the eggs are completely cooked.
8. The eggs should look like lumpy scrambled eggs.
9. Serve Khageena with freshly made parathas.

Parathas

Bread

Ingredients

3 cups wholemeal flour, sieved

1 cup water

1/2 cup plain flour

6 tbsp vegetable oil or melted ghee

Method

1. Mix the flour and half the water and knead the dough well with fingers for 30 minutes, slowly adding the remaining water as you go.
2. Cover with a cloth and set aside for 1 hour
3. Make small balls of the dough and roll each one out as thin as possible with a rolling pin dusted with a little dry flour. Add a few drops of oil or ghee and fold the dough into any shape - circles, squares and triangles are popular. Roll the folded dough out again as thin as possible using little dry plain flour to prevent sticking. Repeat the folding and rolling once more.
4. Heat a pancake pan, and cook the paratha on both sides with a few drops of oil or ghee.

Elaichi Chai

Tea with Cardamom

Ingredients

1/2 cup milk

4 cups water

2 tsp tea leaves, English Breakfast

4 green cardamom, crushed

Method

1. Boil the water in a pan then turn it down, add the cardamom and simmer for 3 minutes.
2. Add the tea leaves and continue to simmer for a further 3 minutes.
3. Add the milk, and turn the heat off.
4. Strain the tea into cups and enjoy.

Meat

The Secunderabad Club is one of the oldest clubs in India. Established in 1878 as an exclusive Club for the nobility of Hyderabad and officers of the British cantonment, it occupies the old hunting lodge of Sir Salar Jung I, once Prime Minister of Hyderabad State. The Club offers excellent dining, a good library, and facilities for many indoor and outdoor sports, with its own cricket field.

This picture relies heavily on watercolour paint with pen and ink used only to highlight the details of the building. The unusual green/blue shade of the building closely resembles the true colour.

- Elizabeth Adams

Daalcha

Lentils with Lamb

Ingredients

3/4 cup Channa daal (yellow split lentils)

1 tsp salt

1/2 tsp turmeric

1 1/2 cups water

500 gms lamb shoulder, diced

2 medium onions, finely chopped

3 tbsp sunflower oil

1 tbsp ginger and garlic paste

4 tbsp chopped tomatoes or 3 fresh tomatoes

1/4 tsp turmeric

1 tsp coriander powder

1 tsp chilli powder

2 bay leaves

3 tbsp tamarind paste

10 curry leaves

2 green chillies

2 tbsp chopped fresh coriander

1 tsp salt, or to taste

Ingredients for grinding:

6 cloves

2" piece cinnamon

4 green cardamom

1 tsp shahzeera

Method

1. Rinse the daal then drain it. Add 1 1/2 cups of water and cook on low heat with the salt and turmeric for 40 minutes, until soft. Add hot water if it seems too thick.

2. For the lamb, in a separate pan heat the oil and fry the onions until golden brown.

3. Add the ginger and garlic and continue frying on low heat for a further 5 minutes.

4. Add the lamb and stir fry well until the lamb is light brown.

5. Add the chopped tomato, turmeric, coriander powder, chilli powder and bay leaves and cook on low heat for 15 minutes.

6. Add the tamarind paste, curry leaves, green chillies, fresh coriander, salt to taste and 1/2 a cup of water and mix well while still on low heat.

7. Add the daal to the lamb and continue cooking for a further 10 minutes on low heat.

8. Grind the cloves, cinnamon, cardamom and shahzeera and add these spices to the pan and cook for a further 5 minuets.

9. Serve with steamed rice.

Korma

Meat in a Spicy Gravy

Ingredients

500 gms diced lamb, chicken or beef

4 tbsp natural youghurt

2 tbsp ginger and garlic paste

1 tsp turmeric

1 tsp chilli powder

2 tsp garam masala

1 tsp salt, or to taste

2 tbsp vegetable oil

2 medium onions, finely chopped

3 cardamom, roughly crushed

6 cloves, roughly crushed

1 tbsp fresh coriander, chopped

1/2 cup water

Juice of 1 lime

Method

1. Marinate the meat in a large bowl with the yogurt, ginger and garlic paste, turmeric, chilli powder, salt, half the garam masala and mix well.
2. Leave this in a covered bowl for at least 4 hours, but preferably overnight in the fridge.
3. Heat the oil and fry the onions in a pan until golden brown.
4. Add the marinated meat to the onions and stir fry well on a high heat for 10 minutes until well browned.
5. Add all the remaining marinade from the bowl, along with 1/2 a cup of water and cover and cook on low heat for 40 minutes.
6. Add the other half of the garam masala, mix well and turn off the heat.
7. Put the korma into a serving dish and add the juice of one lime and freshly chopped coriander.
8. Serve with steamed rice.

Do-Piaza

Chicken with Onions

Ingredients

4 chicken breasts, diced

3 medium onions, finely sliced

3 tsp ginger and garlic paste

3/4 tsp chilli powder

1/2 tsp turmeric

1 tsp salt, or to taste

1 tsp garam masala

2 tbsp freshly chopped coriander

2 tbsp freshly chopped mint leaves

10 cashew nuts

1 tbsp ghee

2 tbsp vegetable oil

1/4 cup water

Juice of 1 lime

Method

1. Heat the oil in a pan and add the chicken and fry well, until it is no longer pink, but do not brown.
2. Continue cooking on a low heat and add the sliced onions, ginger and garlic paste, chilli powder, turmeric and salt.
3. Mix well and cook in a covered pan on low heat for 30 minutes, until the chicken is cooked through.
4. Add the garam masala, cashew nuts, water and ghee. Mix well and continue cooking on low heat for a further 5 minutes.
5. Take off the heat and add the fresh coriander and mint leaves and juice of one lime just before serving.
6. Serve with steamed rice or naan.

Now restored and operated as a luxury hotel, the Faluknama Palace was built over nine years, completed in 1893, and remained the private property of the Nizam until 2000. Set in 32 acres, built in a blend of Victorian and Italian styles, the Palace has a large collection of paintings, manuscripts, statues, jade objects and furniture. The Library, with its carved walnut ceiling, houses one of the finest collections of the Quran in India

This picture is intended to be interesting rather than realistic. The pen and ink detailing has remained strong and attention was given to the lighting at sunset. The pink shading of the building contrasts well with evening lighting and the formal foliage in the garden.

- Elizabeth Adams

Pepper Fry

Ingredients

500 gms diced lamb, beef or chicken

1 medium onion, finely chopped

1 tbsp ginger and garlic paste

1/2 tsp turmeric

1/2 tsp chilli powder

1 tsp salt, or to taste

5 tbsp vegetable oil

1 tbsp black peppercorns

10-12 curry leaves

6-8 cloves

1 tbsp freshly ground black pepper

Method

1. Fry the chopped onions in 2 tbsp of oil until golden brown.
2. Add the ginger and garlic paste and fry on low heat for 5 minutes.
3. Add the meat to the pan, turn the heat up and continue to stir fry for 10 minutes, until the meat is browned.
4. Add the turmeric, chilli powder and salt and stir well.
5. Cover the pan and cook on low heat for 25 minutes, until the meat is cooked and nearly all the juices have evaporated.
6. In a separate pan or wok, add 3 tbsp oil and heat well.
7. Turn the heat down and add the peppercorns, cloves and curry leaves. Fry for 3 minutes.
8. Add the meat and any sauce left in the pan to the wok, and stir fry on high heat for 10 minutes, making sure nothing sticks to the bottom of the pan.
9. Add coarsely ground black pepper and serve.

Dumm ka Kheema

Slow Cooked Steamed Mince

Ingredients

500 gms lamb or beef mince
2 medium onions
2 tsp ginger and garlic paste
1/2 tsp red chilli powder
1/2 tsp turmeric powder
2 tbsp natural yogurt
1 tsp salt, or to taste

Ingredients for the garnist

2 green chillies
8-10 mint leaves
2 tbsp coriander leaves
2 boiled eggs

Method

1. Marinate the mince in ginger and garlic paste, red chilli and turmeric powder and yogurt and set aside for 30 minutes.
2. Heat the oil in a pan and fry thinly sliced onions until soft and golden in colour.
3. Add the marinated mince and stir fry well.
4. Turn the heat down, cover the pan so that the steam does not escape and cook for 30 minutes.
5. Add a little hot water if the mince is sticking to the bottom of the pan.
6. Garnish with sliced green chillies and chopped coriander and mint leaves.
7. Serve with parathas or with steamed rice and Khatti daal.

Pasanda

Dry Lamb with Spices

Ingredients

1 kg lamb, cut into large pieces
1 large onion, finely sliced
3 tsp ginger and garlic paste
2 green chillies, chopped
2 tbsp tomato puree

2 tbsp ghee
1 tsp coriander powder
1/2 tsp turmeric
1 tsp salt, or to taste
1/2 pint full fat natural yogurt

Method

1. Lay the lamb on a board. Cover with cling film and beat crossways and lengthways with a meat mallet.
2. Place the meat along with the yogurt and salt in a dish, mix well and keep covered. Marinate this for 2 hours.
3. In a separate frying pan, heat the oil and fry the onions until golden brown.
4. Add the meat and fry well on both sides.
5. Turn the heat down and add the ginger and garlic paste, green chillies, tomato puree, turmeric and coriander powder and mix well.
6. Cook on low heat for about 40 minutes.
7. Serve with steamed rice.

Pathar ka Gosht

Lamb on a Hot Stone

Ingredients

1 kg leg of lamb
A flat piece of granite

Marinade 1
3 tsp ginger and garlic paste
2 tbsp raw papaya
2 green chillies
Juice of one lime

Marinade 2
3 tbsp vegetable oil
1/2 tsp turmeric
1 tsp red chilli powder
2 tsp garam masala
2 tsp freshly ground black pepper
1 tsp salt, or to taste

Method

1. Make a paste of the raw papaya and green chillies and marinate the lamb in a large bowl with the papaya and green chilli and the ginger and garlic paste and the lime juice for 20 minutes.
2. Add all the ingredients under Marinade 2 to the lamb and mix well and leave in the fridge for 4 hours, or overnight.
3. Place the granite on the barbecue and heat well. Sprinkle a little water on the stone. If it sizzles, it is ready to cook on.
4. Using a pair of tongs, place a few pieces of the marinated lamb at a time on the stone to cook for 7 minutes on each side.
5. Serve on a bed of onion rings and with lime wedges.

Chuggur ka Saalan

Lamb with Tamarind Leaves

Ingredients

1 kg diced lamb shoulder

2 tbsp vegetable oil

1 tsp black mustard seeds

8 cloves

4 green cardamom

4" piece cinnamon

2 medium onions

1 tsp ginger and garlic paste

1/2 tsp turmeric powder

1/2 tsp red chilli powder

1 tsp salt, or to taste

1 cup water

500 gms Chuggur leaves
(tender tamarind leaves)

Method

1. Heat the oil in a pan and add the mustard seeds, cloves, cardamom and cinnamon. Fry on low heat for 3 minutes.
2. Chop the onions finely and add them to the spices in the pan and cook on low heat until translucent and light brown.
3. Add the lamb, turn the heat up, and stir fry well for 10 minutes.
4. Turn the heat down and add the turmeric, chilli powder and salt. Stir in well.
5. Add a cup of hot water, stir and cover and cook for 40 minutes, until the lamb is tender.
6. Finally, wash and add the tamarind leaves and cook uncovered and on low heat for a further 10 minutes until there is a thick sauce left.
7. Serve with parathas, naan or steamed rice.

Laad Bazar is a market for bangles. About a kilometre long, it is named for the Laad, or lacquer, used to decorate the bangles. It is also the place to shop for the many accessories needed for an Indian wedding.

The bangles were drawn in pencil first and many coats of paint were applied to achieve the depth of colour. The light hitting the bangles was then applied, followed by the pen and ink outlining. Finally, a coat of clear sparkle paint was applied across much of the painting.

- Elizabeth Adams

Kheema Methi

Mince with Fenugreek

Ingredients

500 gms lamb or beef mince

2 medium onions, chopped finely

2 tsp ginger and garlic paste

1 tsp salt, or to taste

3/4 tsp turmeric

1/2 tsp chilli powder

1 tsp coriander powder

3 tbsp tomato puree or 4 fresh ripe tomatoes, chopped

6 tbsp dry fenugreek leaves or 1 bunch fresh fenugreek leaves, washed well

1/4 cup water

2 tbsp vegetable oil

Method

1. Heat the oil in a pan and fry the onions until golden brown.
2. Add the mince to the pan and fry well until browned.
3. Turn the heat low and add the ginger and garlic paste and stir fry well for 5 minutes.
4. Add the turmeric, chilli powder, coriander powder and salt and continue to stir fry on low heat for a further 5 minutes.
5. Add the tomatoes/puree and 1/4 cup water, stir well, cover and cook on low heat for 30 minutes.
6. Stir in the fenugreek leaves and leave on low heat for a further 10 minutes.

Ambade or Chukke ki Bhaji with Gosht

Green Leafy Vegetable with Lamb

Ingredients

1 kg diced lamb shoulder
2 tsp ginger and garlic paste
1/2 tsp turmeric
1/2 tsp chilli powder
1 tsp coriander powder
1 tsp salt, or to taste
1/4 cup hot water

300 gms ambada (red sorrel) leaves
300 gms chukka (green sorrel) leaves
2 ripe tomatoes
2 tbsp vegetable oil
2 medium onions
10-12 curry leaves
2 tbsp fresh coriander

Method

1. Marinate the lamb in the ginger and garlic paste, turmeric, chilli powder, coriander powder and salt and set aside while doing the next steps.
2. Wash the ambada and chukka leaves well and put into a large pan.
3. Chop the tomatoes and add them to the leaves and cover and steam on low heat for 30 minutes until they soften completely.
4. Use a food processor to make the leaves and tomatoes into a smooth paste and set aside.
5. Chop the onions finely and fry them in a heavy bottomed pan on low heat until soft and golden brown.
6. Add the marinated lamb to the onions and stir fry well for 5 minutes on a higher heat, making sure the sauce does not stick to the bottom of the pan.
7. Turn the heat down, add 1/4 cup hot water, stir well, cover and cook for 45 minutes.
8. Add the ambada and chukka leaf paste to the lamb, stir well and take off the heat.
9. Add 2 tbsp freshly chopped coriander just before serving.
10. Serve with steamed white rice.

Masala Chops

Spicy Lamb Cutlets

Ingredients

16 lamb cutlets

1 medium onion, finely chopped

1/2 tsp turmeric

1 tsp freshly ground black pepper

1 tsp salt, or to taste

2 tsp ginger and garlic paste

1/2 tsp garam masala

10 peppercorns

10 cloves

2 green cardamom

4 tbsp vegetable oil

Method

1. Marinate the lamb cutlets in the chopped onion, turmeric, pepper, salt, ginger and garlic paste and garam masala and leave covered for 2 hours.
2. Heat the oil in a large frying pan and turn down the heat before frying the peppercorns, cloves and cardamom for 2 minutes, until the aromas are released.
3. Continue cooking on low heat and add the cutlets to the pan and fry well on both sides.
4. Cover and cook on low heat for 20 minutes.
5. Take off the lid, turn up the heat to ensure the cutlets are brown on both sides just before serving.

Bhuna Gosht

Dry Roasted Lamb

Ingredients

1 kg diced boneless leg of lamb

2 medium onions, finely sliced

2 tsp ginger and garlic paste

1 tsp turmeric powder

1/2 tsp red chilli powder

1 tsp garam masala

1 cup water

Juice of one lime

2 tbsp fresh coriander leaves

2 green chillies

2 tbsp vegetable oil

Method

1. Heat the oil in a large pan and fry the onion on low heat until they are soft and golden brown.
2. Add the lamb and stir fry on a high heat until the lamb is well browned.
3. Turn the heat down and add the ginger and garlic paste, turmeric and chilli powder and stir fry well for 5 minutes, adding a little water if the spices begin to stick to the bottom of the pan.
4. Add a cup of hot water, stir well and cover the pan and cook on low heat for 40 minutes, until the lamb is tender.
5. Take off the lid, add garam masala and stir fry on a high heat for 10 minutes, and until most of the gravy has evaporated.
6. Garnish with lime juice and slit green chillies.

Dhaggi ka Gosht

Spicy Shredded Lamb

Ingredients

1 kg diced leg of lamb

4 tsp khus khus (poppy seeds)

2 tsp shahzeera

6 cloves

4" piece cinnamon

6 green cardamom

1 tsp turmeric

1 tsp chilli powder

1 tsp salt, or to taste

3/4 cup water

4 tbsp vegetable oil

Method

1. Roast the poppy seeds, shahzeera, cloves, cinnamon and cardamom in a dry frying pan on low heat.

2. Marinate the meat in the above spices and leave covered for 2 hours.

3. Add salt, turmeric and chilli powder to the meat and mix well.

4. Put the meat into a pan with 3/4 cup water. Mix well and cover and cook on low heat for 20 minutes, until the water has evaporated.

5. Once cooled a little bit, pound the meat with a rolling pin so that it shreds into thin strips.

6. Heat the oil in a separate pan or wok, add the pounded meat and stir fry for 20 minutes and until crisp.

Chicken 65

Ingredients

750 gms chicken breast, diced
3 tbsp natural yogurt
3 tsp ginger and garlic paste
Juice of 2 limes
3/4 tsp chilli powder
1/2 tsp turmeric

1 tsp coriander powder
1/2 tsp cumin powder
2 tsp cornflour
12-14 curry leaves
6 tbsp vegetable oil

Method

1. Marinate the diced chicken in yogurt, ginger and garlic paste and lime juice and leave overnight in the fridge.

2. Heat the oil in in a large pan or wok, and add the chicken and stir fry it well on a high heat for 10 minutes.

3. Turn the heat down and add the chilli powder, turmeric, coriander and cumin powder and continue stir frying for a further 10 minutes, making sure the spices do not stick to the bottom of the pan.

4. Add the cornflour and curry leaves and stir well while frying for another 10 minutes until the curry leaves and chicken are crisp.

Kofta Curry

Meatball Curry

Ingredients

500 gms mince, lamb or beef

1 small and 1 large onion, finely chopped

1 tbsp ginger and garlic paste

6 ripe tomatoes, chopped or 4 tbsp tomato puree

1 tsp coriander powder

1/2 tsp turmeric

2 tsp garam masala

1 tsp chilli powder

1/4 tsp nutmeg

2 bay leaves

2 tbsp freshly chopped coriander leaves

1 medium egg

1 tsp salt, or to taste

2 tbsp vegetable oil

2 cups water

Method for the Kofta

1. Put the mince in a large mixing bowl.
2. Add the small chopped onion, fresh coriander, 1 tsp garam masala, 1/2 tsp chilli powder, 1 egg and mix well.
3. Make into small balls (koftas) and keep aside in the fridge while the curry is being made.

Method for the curry:

1. Heat the oil in a pan and fry the chopped large onion until golden brown.
2. Add the tomatoes, turmeric, chilli powder, coriander powder, nutmeg and bay leaves and fry on low heat for 15 minutes. Add 2 tbsp water to make a smooth paste.
3. Add 2 cups of boiling water and turn up the heat.
4. Drop the koftas into the boiling sauce one at a time.
5. Cook for a further 20 minutes on low heat.
6. Add the garam masala and freshly chopped coriander just before serving.

Nargisi Kofta

Meatballs in a Spicy Gravy

Ingredients for the Kofta

4 eggs, hard boiled

1 kg mince, lamb, beef or chicken

2 tsp ginger and garlic paste

1/2 tsp red chilli powder

1/2 tsp turmeric

2 tsp garam masala

1 tbsp lime juice

2 green chillies, finely chopped

2 tbsp fresh coriander leaves, finely chopped

2 tbsp fresh mint leaves, finely chopped

1 tsp salt, or to taste

10 tbsp vegetable oil

Ingredients for the gravy

4" piece cinnamon

4 cloves

1/2 tsp black peppercorns

1 tsp shahzeera (caraway seeds)

2 onions

2 tsp ginger and garlic paste

1 tbsp tomato puree

1/2 tsp chilli powder

1/2 tsp turmeric

2 tsp garam masala

10 almonds

1 tsp salt, or to taste

1/2 cup water

Method for the Kofta:

1. Soak the almonds in warm water and keep aside for 3 hours, peel and grind into a paste and save.
2. Boil the eggs so that they are hard boiled and keep aside. Peel and leave whole.
3. Put the mince into a large bowl and add the ginger and garlic paste, chilli powder, turmeric, garam masala, salt, lime juice, finely chopped green chillies, coriander and mint and mix well.
4. Wrap each boiled egg with a thick layer of mince, press firmly making sure it stays on.
5. Heat the oil in a non-stick frying pan and fry them until well browned.
6. Set aside on kitchen paper to drain any excess oil.

Method for the gravy:

1. Using a heavy bottom pan, use any remaining oil from the frying pan, heat well.
2. Turn the heat down and fry the cinnamon, cloves, peppercorns and caraway seeds for one minute.
3. Chop the onions and add them to the spices and fry them on low heat until soft and golden brown.
4. Add the ginger and garlic paste and fry for a further minute.
5. Add the tomato puree, chilli powder, turmeric, garam masala, ground almonds and salt and cook on low heat, stirring well for 10 minutes.
6. Add half a cup of hot water to make a thick gravy.
7. Cut the koftas into halves and serve with the gravy on a bed of steamed rice.
8. Garnish with a few fresh coriander leaves just before serving.

Sharifabee's Mother's Whole Chicken

This was cooked by Sharifabee's mother for us for Eid every year

Ingredients for the Kofta

1 whole organic chicken

1 cup full fat natural yogurt

1 tsp turmeric

1 tsp chilli powder

2 tbsp ginger and garlic paste

2 tbsp fresh coriander, chopped

2 tbsp fresh mint leaves, chopped

2 medium onions

4 tbsp vegetable oil

8 eggs

Juice of 2 limes

Ingredients for grinding

Dry roast the following and grind into a dry powder
or into a paste with a little water

2 tbsp poppy seeds

2 tbsp chirongi nuts

1tsp shahzeera (caraway seeds)

6 green cardamom

6 cloves

2" piece cinnamon

Method

1. Chop the onions finely and fry them in 2 tbsp vegetable oil on low heat until they are soft and golden brown. Set aside.
2. In a bowl, mix together the yogurt, turmeric, chilli powder, ground spices, ginger and garlic paste and browned onions to make the marinade.
3. Marinate the chicken well in the above and cover with cling film and set aside for 4 hours, or preferably overnight.
4. Preheat the oven to 180°C.
5. Brush the chicken with the remaining 2 tbsp of vegetable oil, baste well and cover with foil and cook in the oven for 1 hour and 30 minutes, or time it according to the weight of the chicken.
6. Baste the chicken every half hour and cook uncovered for the last 20 minutes.
7. Hard boil the eggs, let them cool before peeling them. Leave whole.
8. Once the chicken is ready, put it in a serving dish, along with all the sauce around it.
9. Put the boiled eggs into the cavity of the chicken and pour a little sauce into the cavity to cover the eggs.
10. Add the juice of two limes and chopped coriander and mint leaves to the chicken just before serving.
11. Best eaten with steamed white rice.

Mahakhaliya

Lamb in a Rich Gravy

Ingredients

1 kg lamb

3 onions

4 cloves garlic

3" piece ginger

6 tbsp chopped tomato

3 tbsp tamarind paste

1 tsp cumin seed

1/2 tsp turmeric

1 tsp chilli powder

2 tbsp desiccated coconut

10-12 curry leaves

salt to taste

veg oil

1 cup water

Ingredients for grinding

1 1/2 tsp coriander

1 1/2 tsp zeera

2 tsp sesame seed

2 tbsp roasted peanuts

1 tbsp khus khus (poppy seed)

Ingredients to roast and grind

1 onion, finely chopped

2 black (big) cardamom

Method

1. Heat the oil, add cumin seeds, curry leaves, onions and fry well until soft and golden brown.
2. Add the lamb and fry for 10 minutes until well browned.
3. Stir in the ginger and garlic paste and continue cooking on low heat for 5 minutes.
4. Add chopped tomatoes, mix well and cook for a further 10 minutes.
5. Continue cooking on low heat and add the ground spices stirring well all the time so that the spices do not get stuck to the bottom of the pan.
6. Add turmeric, chilli powder, tamarind and desiccated coconut and add up to a cup of boiling water and mix well and cook for a further 20 minutes until the gravy is thick.

Top Tip: For smooth gravy, add 2 tbsp peanut butter instead of the peanuts

Haleem

Lamb with Bulgar Wheat

Ingredients

1 kg lamb (shoulder), diced

2 tbsp ginger and garlic paste

1 cup full fat natural youghurt

1 1/2 tsp turmeric

1 tsp chilli powder

4 tbsp vegetable oil

10 medium onions, finely sliced

4 cloves

4 cardamom

2 cups bulgar wheat

1 tsp salt

1 cup water

Ingredients for grinding

2 tsp shahzeera

8 green cardamom

8 cloves

6" piece cinnamon

Ingredients for the garnish

1 bunch fresh mint leaves

crisp fried onion slices

2 limes, each cut into 4 wedges

4 tbsp ghee

Method

1. Marinate the lamb in the yogurt, ginger, garlic, turmeric, chilli powder and ground spices in a large bowl for at least 4 hours, but preferably overnight.
2. Heat the oil in a large pan and fry the onions until golden brown and crisp.
3. Remove 3/4 of the onions onto kitchen paper for later use.
4. Add the 4 cloves and cardamom and continue to fry on low heat for 5 minutes.
5. Add the lamb, turn up the heat and stir well until well browned.
6. Put all the remaining marinade into the pan and mix in well.
7. Turn the heat down, cover and cook for 45 minutes, stirring occasionally to make sure nothing is stuck to the bottom of the pan.
8. In a separate bowl, pour one cup of boiling water onto the bulgar wheat and salt and cover. Fork it so that it is fluffy. Leave for 15 minutes.
9. Add the bulgar wheat to the lamb and mix it in gently but well. Add a little more hot water if necessary, to get a nearly dry consistency.
10. Drain excess oil on kitchen paper and put the crispy onions on to a serving plate.
11. Wash and pat dry the fresh mint leaves and arrange them on a plate together with the lime wedges.
12. Melt the ghee and serve it from a small jug.
13. To eat, help yourself to a portion of the haleem, add the garnish of ghee, a few crisp onions, mint leaves and a squeeze of lime.

Tahiri

Mildly Flavoured Lamb and Vegetables with Rice

Ingredients

500 gms diced lamb (shoulder or leg)

2 medium onions, finely chopped

2 tsp ginger and garlic paste

1/2 tsp turmeric

2 tsp coriander powder

1 tsp chilli powder

1 tsp garam masala

2 tbsp vegetable oil

2 cups water

1 1/2 cups basmati rice

1 tbsp vegetable oil

3 green cardamom

6 cloves

2" piece cinnamon

2 bay leaves

1/2 cauliflower

1/4 cabbage

3 carrots

1/2 cup peas

Method

1. Heat the oil and fry the chopped onions until soft and golden brown.
2. Add the lamb to the onions and stir fry well for 10 minutes.
3. Turn the heat to low and add the ginger and garlic paste while stirring well.
4. Continue to cook on a low flame and add turmeric, chilli and coriander powder and stir fry well, making sure the spices do not stick to the bottom of the pan.
5. Add two cups of hot water, add the garam masala and stir well, cover and cook for 25 minutes.
6. Rinse and pre-soak the rice and set aside for 20 minutes.
7. In a separate large pan, heat one tbsp oil and turn the heat down before frying the cardamom, cloves, cinnamon and bay leaves for 5 minutes.
8. Wash and cut the vegetables and add them to the whole spices and stir gently.
9. Drain the water from the rice and add the rice to the vegetables and mix gently.
10. Add the lamb curry to the pan of vegetables and rice, stir gently.
11. Add hot water, if necessary, making sure there is twice as much liquid as the rice (ie 3 cups from the lamb curry and any additional water).
12. Cover and cook on low heat for 15 minutes, until the rice and vegetables are tender, but not over-cooked.

Shikampoor Kebab

Ingredients

600 gms lamb mince

6 tbsp channa daal

4 tbsp water

1/4 cup yogurt, hung

3 medium onions, chopped

1 tbsp fresh mint leaves, chopped

2 green chillies, finely chopped

2 tbsp fresh coriander leaves, chopped

1 tsp mace powder

1/2 tsp red chilli powder

2 tsp garam masala

2 tsp salt, or to taste

2 egg whites

2 tbsp plain flour

12 tbsp vegetable oil

Method

1. Rinse the channa daal and cook it together with the mince and 4 tbsp water for 30 minutes, until cooked and dry.
2. Hang the yogurt in a muslin cloth to let the water drain out completely.
3. Chop one onion and the mint leaves finely and add these to the yogurt, mix well and save.
4. Heat 3 tbsp of oil in a pan and fry the remaining two onions on low heat until soft and golden brown and save in a bowl.
5. Once the mince is cooled, put it in a food processor and mix it well until you get a fine paste. Put this in a large bowl.
6. Add the browned onions, green chillies, coriander leaves, mace, chilli powder, garam masala, salt, egg whites and plain flour to the mince and mix very well.
7. Take a little mince mixture and roll it into a tight ball to fit in your palm.
8. Make a deep groove with your thumb.
9. Add half a spoon of the yogurt/onion/mint mixture, and seal the kebab.
10. Flatten the kebab slightly. It should now be a little long and slightly flat.
11. Heat the oil in a large frying pan and fry the kebabs, few at a time, on low heat, until well browned on both sides.
12. Serve on a bed of onion rings with lime wedges.

Shammi Kebab

Ingredients

500 gms leg of lamb, diced
1 medium onion
1 tsp ginger and garlic paste
1/4 cup channa daal
1/2 tsp turmeric
1/2 tsp chilli powder
1 tsp salt, or to taste
1/2 cup water
1 1/2 tsp garam masala
3 tbsp freshly chopped coriander

2 tbsp freshly chopped mint leaves
1 fresh green chilli, seeded and finely chopped (optional)
1 egg
6 tbsp vegetable oil
1 medium mild onion, cut into rings
1 lime, cut into wedges

Method

1. Put the lamb, onions, channa daal, ginger and garlic paste, turmeric, chilli powder, salt and hot water in a pan, mix well, cover and cook on low heat for 40 minutes.
2. Uncover and continue cooking until all the liquid has evaporated.
3. After the lamb mixture has cooled down, add the garam masala, fresh coriander, mint, green chilli (optional) and one beaten egg.
4. Put this mixture into a food processor and whisk for 5 minutes, until well mixed.
5. In a large frying pan, heat the oil and then turn it down to low heat.
6. Make small balls and flatten them into approximately 2" cakes and fry them until brown on both sides.
7. Serve on a bed of onion rings with lime wedges and green chutney.

The Mecca Masjid is one of the largest mosques in India. Legend has it that soil from Mecca was used to make some of the bricks for the central arch, giving the mosque its name. Started by the 5th Qutb Shahi ruler, Muhammad Qutb Quli Shah, in 1694, construction halted when he died in 1612, before being completed in 1694 by the Moghul emperor Aurangzeb after he had conquered the Golconda Sultanate. A desire on his part to limit expense apparently resulted in the oddly stunted minarets, which hardly rise above the main building.

The watercolour paint was applied in several coats in order to obtain the golden hue of the building. The sky and street have been simplified and the crowds were not included so that the pen and ink would stand out.

- Elizabeth Adams

Boti Kebab

Ingredients

1 kg diced leg or shoulder of lamb

2 tbsp ginger and garlic paste

1 tsp salt

4 tbsp lime juice

3 tbsp papaya, mashed

5 tbsp natural yogurt

1 tsp cumin powder

1 tsp white pepper

1 tsp green cardamom powder

1 tsp red chilli powder

3 tbsp vegetable oil

2 tbsp melted ghee

Method

1. Dice the lamb into large pieces (2" x 2")
2. Marinate the lamb in a large bowl with the ginger and garlic paste, salt and lime juice for 30 minutes.
3. Add all the remaining ingredients, except the ghee to the lamb, mix gently but well and leave to marinate for at least 2 hours, or overnight in the fridge.
4. Skewer the lamb pieces.
5. Grill the kebabs, basting the meat with the melted ghee from time to time for approximately 20 minutes, until cooked.
6. You could barbecue them as well.
7. Serve with a mint chutney or raita.

Fish & Seafood

The Secunderabad Sailing Club, actually the Sailing Annexe to the Secunderabad Club, is one of the oldest sailing clubs in India. Set on the edge of the picturesque, 5.7 km², Hussein Sagar Lake, it hosts the Hyderabad Sailing Week regatta every summer.

The original photo of the lake was very dark as the sun had already set so some artistic license was taken and a sunset over the lake was added to create more interest. The colours in the lake were deliberately exaggerated with a strong watercolour wash.

- Elizabeth Adams

Chirala Mackerel

Ingredients

4 whole mackerel, gutted and washed

1 tsp turmeric

1 tsp cumin powder

2 tbsp tomato puree

1 tbsp tamarind paste

2 tbsp coconut cream

1/2 tsp salt

2 tsp black mustard seed

12 curry leaves

2 tbsp vegetable oil

Method

1. Gut and wash the fish and pat dry and lay them side by side on a large plate. You can ask the fishmonger to take the head off too if you prefer.
2. Using a sharp knife, make three light slits on both sides of the fish.
3. Put the turmeric, cumin powder, tomato puree, tamarind paste, coconut cream and salt in a small bowl and mix well to make a thick paste.
4. Put this paste into the cavity of the fish and smear some of it on to the skin on both sides, letting some penetrate through the slits in the skin.
5. Heat the oil in a large frying pan and turn the heat down before adding the mustard seed and curry leaves to the pan. Fry for 2 minutes before frying the fish two by two for 7 minutes on both sides. Turn the heat down so as not to burn the skin.
6. You can also grill or barbecue this fish but remember to add 1 tbsp of oil to the marinade.

Khatti Macchi

Fish with Tamarind

Ingredients

1 kg firm fish, eg monk fish or salmon

3 tbsp vegetable oil

1 medium onion

4 ripe tomatoes, chopped or 2 tbsp tomato puree

2 tbsp tamarind paste

1 tsp salt, or to taste

10 cloves garlic, sliced

1 cup water

Ingredients for grinding

2 whole red dried chillies

1 tsp fenugreek seed

1 tsp cumin seed

1 1/2 tsp coriander seed

Ingredients for the garnish

1 tsp black mustard seed

1 tsp urud daal

10-12 curry leaves

Method

1. Heat the oil in a large pan, and fry the black mustard seed, urud daal and curry leaves on low heat for 5 minutes.

2. Add the onions and fry them until they are soft and golden brown.

3. Add the tomatoes, tamarind paste, salt and 1/2 a cup of boiling water and continue simmering on low heat for 10 minutes.

4. Slice the garlic cloves in half lengthways and add to the sauce.

5. In a small pan, fry the spices for grinding in 2 drops of oil and on low heat for 3 minutes.

6. Grind these to a fine mixture and add it to the sauce. Mix well and continue to let it simmer for another 10 minutes.

7. Add the fish, cover and cook for 15 minutes.

8. Serve with steamed rice.

Sharifabee's Crabs

Ingredients

4 whole crabs, cleaned and washed or 16 large crab claws

2 medium onions, finely chopped

2 tsp ginger and garlic paste

1/2 tsp turmeric

1 1/2 tsp cumin powder

1 tsp chilli powder

1 tsp salt, or to taste

8 ripe tomatoes or 4 tbsp tomato puree

1 can coconut milk

1 cup water

Method

1. Have the fishmonger clean the crabs well. If using claws, please wash well under cold water with a brush and set aside.
2. Heat the oil in a large pan and fry the onions until they are golden brown.
3. Turn the heat down and add the ginger and garlic paste, and fry for a further 5 minutes.
4. Add the turmeric, cumin and chilli powders and salt. Mix well and continue cooking on low heat for a further 5 minutes.
5. Add the tomatoes and coconut milk, stir well and let it simmer for another 10 minutes, until the sauce is smooth.
6. Add up to one cup boiling water to make a thick gravy.
7. Add the crabs/ claws to the sauce, cover and simmer for a further 30 minutes.
8. Serve with steamed rice.

Eggs, Lentils & Vegetables

Kutt

Eggs in a Tomato Gravy

Ingredients

1 1/2 kg ripe tomatoes

3 tbsp grated coconut (fresh, if possible)

1 tsp salt, to taste

1 tsp cumin powder

1 tsp coriander powder

3 bay leaves

2 green chillies

5 cloves garlic, sliced

1 tsp gram flour or cornflour

4 hard boiled eggs

Ingredients for the garnish

1 tbsp sunflower oil

1 tsp cumin seed

10-12 curry leaves

Method

1. Wash, cut and cook the tomatoes in a large pan along with the grated coconut, cumin, chilli powder and salt for 30 minutes.

2. Take it off the heat and let it cool down. Then blend well in a food processor and sieve it back into the pan.

3. Add bay leaves, green chillies and sliced garlic and bring to the boil, then turn down and continue cooking on low heat for 5 minutes.

4. Mix the flour in a little cold water and add to the pan to thicken the sauce and cook for a further 5-7 minutes on low heat.

5. Boil the eggs, let them cool then cut them in half lengthways and add them to the sauce.

6. For the garnish, heat the oil in a separate pan, and add the cumin seed and curry leaves and fry on low heat for 3 minutes.

7. Add the garnish to the sauce just before serving with steamed rice.

Khatti Daal

Lentils

Ingredients

1 cup Masoor daal (red lentils)
1/2 tsp turmeric
1/2 tsp chilli powder
1 1/2 cups water
1 1/2 tbsp tamarind paste
3 tomatoes, halved
4 green chillies, whole
1 bunch fresh coriander, roughly chopped

Ingredients for the garnish

1 tbsp ghee or sunflower oil
1 tsp mustard seed
10-12 curry leaves, fresh or dried
3 cloves garlic, sliced

Method

1. Rinse the daal in cold water and put it into a pan with the water, turmeric and chilli powder.
2. Bring it to the boil then turn down, cover and cook on low heat for 30 minutes.
3. Add the tamarind, tomatoes, green chillies and coriander and let it cook on low heat for a further 10 minutes.
4. For the garnish, heat the ghee or oil in a separate pan, add the mustard seed, curry leaves and garlic and fry on low heat until the garlic is light brown.
5. Put the daal into a serving bowl, and add the garnish on top just before serving.
6. Serve with steamed rice.

Constructed by the Birla Foundation, the Birla Mandir sits on one of the twin hills of Hyderabad, 85m above the surrounding land. This white marble edifice combines North Indian and South Indian styles of temple architecture and houses an imposing 3m high idol of Lord Venkateshwara, a form of the Hindu god Vishnu, in black granite.

The pen and ink has been softened with grey watercolour paint to avoid a stark contrast between the white building and the black pen. The dense foliage in the foreground provides a good contrast with the building.

- Elizabeth Adams

Meethi Daal

Lentils

Ingredients

1 cup Toor daal (yellow lentils)
1/2 tsp turmeric
1/2 tsp chilli powder
1 1/2 cups water

Ingredients for the garnish

1 tbsp ghee or sunflower oil
10-12 curry leaves
1 1/2 tsp cumin seed
2 whole dried red chillies
3 cloves garlic, sliced

Method

1. Rinse the daal in cold water, drain and then add to the water, turmeric and chilli powder in a saucepan.
2. Bring it to the boil, then turn it down and cook on low heat for 40 minutes, adding a little hot water if it seems to be getting too thick.
3. For the garnish, heat the ghee or oil in a separate pan, then add the curry leaves and cumin seed until light brown. Add the dried red chillies and sliced garlic just before turning off the heat.
4. Pour the garnish on top of the daal just before serving.
5. Serve with steamed rice.

Sambhar

Spiced Lentils with Vegetables

Ingredients

1 cup Toor daal
2 cups water
1 tsp salt, or to taste
1/2 tsp turmeric
2 tsp sambhar powder
2 tbsp tamarind paste

1/2 white radish
2 medium carrots
1 aubergine
12 green beans
1/2 cup peas

Ingredients for the garnish

1 tbsp vegetable oil
1 tbsp ghee
2 tsp black mustard seed
10-12 curry leaves

Method

1. Wash and rinse the daal and pressure cook it with two cups of water, salt and turmeric for 10 minutes. Turn the heat off. Uncover once it has cooled completely.
2. Chop and use any two preferred vegetables into bite-sized pieces.
3. Turn the heat back on low.
4. Add the vegetables to the daal and mix gently.
5. Add the sambhar powder and tamarind paste and mix well and let it simmer for 15 minutes, until the vegetables are *al dente*.
6. Stir gently while cooking so that the daal does not stick to the bottom of the pan, adding a little hot water if necessary.
7. In a separate pan, heat the oil and turn the heat down, then add the mustard seeds and curry leaves and cook for 1/2 a minute.
8. Put the sambhar into a serving dish and add the garnish just before serving.
9. Serve with steamed rice.

Baghare Baingan or Mirchi ka Saalan

Aubergines or Chillies in a Thick Spicy Sauce

Ingredients

10 baby aubergines, washed and split in half keeping the stalk end intact

or

10 large whole mild green chillies, washed

4 tbsp vegetable oil

1 tsp black mustard seed

1 tsp cumin seed

10-12 curry leaves

2 medium onions, finely chopped

3 ripe tomatoes, chopped or 2 tbsp tomato puree

1/2 tsp turmeric

1/2 tsp chilli powder

5 tbsp smooth peanut butter

3 tbsp tamarind paste

Salt to taste

1/2 cup water

Juice of one lime

Ingredients to roast and grind

3 tsp coriander seed

3 tsp cumin seed

2 tbsp desiccated coconut

3 tsp sesame seed

Method

1. Roast the spices listed under 'To roast and grind' in a frying pan on low heat for 3 mins and grind into a fine powder. Keep aside.

2. In a large pan, heat the oil and turn the heat down before adding the mustard and cumin seeds and curry leaves. Fry for 3 minutes.

3. Add the chopped onions and fry on low heat until soft and golden brown.

4. Add the tomatoes, turmeric and chilli powder and continue cooking while stirring well for a further 5 minutes.

5. Add the peanut butter, tamarind, salt and 1/2 a cup of hot water and mix well and cook on low heat for 15 minutes.

6. Add the ground spices and cook for a further 10 minutes.

7. Add the baby aubergines or whole green chillies and cook covered for 15 minutes.

8. Serve with steamed rice or lamb biryani.

Rasam

Lentil Soup

Ingredients

1/2 cup red lentils

3 cups water

1/2 tsp turmeric

1 tsp salt, or to taste

2 tbsp tamarind paste

6 cloves garlic

2 tbsp fresh roughly ground black pepper

3 tomatoes

3 tbsp fresh coriander leaves

Ingredients for the garnish

1 tbsp vegetable oil

1 tsp black mustard seed

10-12 curry leaves

Method

1. Wash and rinse the lentils, and cook them in 3 cups of boiling water along with the turmeric and salt for 30 minutes, until well cooked, almost mashed.

2. Add the tamarind paste and continue cooking on low heat.

3. Add more boiling water to the pan to make up to a litre of liquid.

4. Let it simmer on low heat for the next 15 minutes while doing the next steps.

5. Peel the garlic and break them roughly in a pestle and mortar and add this to the rasam.

6. Grind the black peppercorns in the same pestle and mortar and add to the rasam.

7. Cut the tomatoes in halves and add them and the fresh coriander leaves to the rasam.

8. In a separate pan, heat the oil and turn the heat down before adding the mustard seeds and curry leaves. Fry these for 2 minutes before adding the garnish on top of the liquid.

9. Mix well and serve this with steamed rice in a bowl.

10. Rasam can also be served in a cup to sip during the meal.

Dumm Aloo

Spicy Steamed Potatoes

Ingredients

400 gms baby potatoes

2 tsp root ginger, finely chopped

2 green chillies

2 bay leaves

5 green cardamom

2 x 2" pieces cinnamon

4 tbsp tomato puree

1/4 tsp garam masala

1 tsp salt, or to taste

2 tbsp ghee

1 tbsp vegetable oil

1/2 cup water

1 tbsp freshly chopped coriander

Method

1. Heat the ghee and oil in a pan.
2. Fry the potatoes until the skin is slightly crisp.
3. Turn the heat down and add all the remaining ingredients and mix well.
4. Cover, making sure the pan is sealed well, and cook on low heat for 30 minutes.
5. Add freshly chopped coriander just before serving.

Gawar ki Phalli

Beans

Ingredients

250 gms cluster (Gawar) beans, or use runner beans if you cannot find cluster beans

2 potatoes

1 medium onions, finely chopped

2 ripe tomatoes, chopped

1/2 tsp turmeric powder

1/2 tsp red chilli powder

2 tbsp vegetable oil

1/2 tsp salt

Ingredients to grind

2 tbsp sesame seed, dry roasted

1 small green chilli

1" piece root ginger

3 cloves garlic

Method

1. Wash and string the beans, and cut them diagonally into 1/2" pieces.
2. Heat the oil in a pan, and fry the onions until soft and light brown.
3. Turn the heat down and add turmeric and chilli powder and stir well for 2 minutes.
4. Add the chopped tomatoes and stir well, and continue cooking on low heat until the oil comes to the surface.
5. Peel and dice the potatoes into small pieces and add to the pan and mix well. Continue cooking on low heat for 5-7 minutes, adding a little water if the spices begin to stick to the bottom of the pan.
6. Add the beans, mix well and cover and cook for 5 minutes.
7. Dry roast the sesame seeds in a frying pan and grind this together with the green chilli, ginger and garlic into a smooth paste.
8. Check that the potatoes and beans are cooked through, and then add the ground paste and mix in well 2 minutes before turning off the heat.
9. Serve with khatti daal, korma and steamed rice.

Aloo Methi

Potatoes with Fenugreek

Ingredients

4 medium sized potatoes
1 medium onion, finely chopped
1 tsp ginger and garlic paste
1/2 tsp turmeric
1/2 tsp coriander powder
1/2 tsp cumin powder

1/2 tsp chilli powder
1 tsp salt, or to taste
3 tbsp water
6 tbsp fenugreek (methi) leaves, fresh or dried

Method

1. Peel, wash and dice the potatoes.
2. Parboil the potatoes, drain and set aside.
3. In a separate pan, heat the oil and fry the onions on low heat until they are soft and golden brown.
4. Add the ginger and garlic paste and continue stir frying on low heat for a further 3 minutes.
5. Add the turmeric, coriander, cumin and chilli powder and stir fry for 3 minutes more.
6. Add salt and 3 tbsp water and cover and cook on low heat for 5 mins.
7. Add the parboiled potatoes and fenugreek leaves and cook for 10 minutes until the potatoes are fully cooked.
8. Turn the heat up gently and stir fry well for 5 minutes until the fenugreek is slightly crisp.

Biryani & Rice

Biryani

Spiced Lamb with Rice

Ingredients

1 kg lamb (shoulder), diced
2 tbsp ginger and garlic paste
1 cup full fat natural yogurt
1 1/2 tsp turmeric
1 tsp chilli powder
4 tbsp vegetable oil
6 medium onions, finely sliced
4 cloves
4 cardamom

20 cashew nuts, optional
1 bunch fresh coriander leaves, roughly chopped
Juice of 1 lime
A generous pinch of saffron
2 tbsp ghee
2 cups of basmati rice
Water

Ingredients to grind

2 tsp shahzeera
8 green cardamom
8 cloves
6" piece cinnamon

Method

1. Marinate the lamb in the yogurt, ginger, garlic, turmeric, chilli powder and ground spices in a large bowl for at least 4 hours, but preferably overnight.
2. Rinse and soak the rice in cold water for an hour.
3. Heat the oil in a large pan and fry the onions until golden brown.
4. Remove half the onions onto kitchen paper for later use.
5. Add the 4 cloves, cardamom and cashew nuts (optional) and continue to fry on low heat for 5 minutes.
6. Add the lamb, turn up the heat and stir well until well browned.
7. Put all the remaining marinade into the pan and mix in well.
8. Turn the heat down, cover and cook for 45 minutes, stirring occasionally to make sure nothing is stuck to the bottom of the pan.
9. Drain the rice, and add it on top of the lamb. Add boiling water just to cover the rice.
10. Add the fresh coriander leaves, lime juice, saffron and ghee on top and cover and cook on low heat for a further 20 minutes, until the rice is done.
11. In a separate frying pan, heat one tbsp of oil and fry the remaining browned onions until they are crisp. Drain again on kitchen paper.
12. Serve the biryani with the crisp onions scattered on top.

Monda Market was established over a hundred years ago to serve the military town of Secunderabad, as it then was. For many years it was the largest vegetable market in the twin cities, but since the wholesale side moved out in 1998, it is said that now one can buy almost anything here.

This painting relies on watercolours and very little pen and ink detailing. The crowds were excluded to allow the fruit and vegetables to stand out.

- Elizabeth Adams

Andhra Biryani

Spiced Chicken with Rice

Ingredients

1 kg chicken thighs and breasts
6 tbsp vegetable oil
4 medium onions
2 tbsp ginger and garlic paste
1 tsp turmeric
1 tsp salt, or to taste
3 tsp garam masala
4 green chillies, sliced in half
Water
2 tbsp ghee

2 cups basmati rice, rinsed and soaked

Ingredients to grind

14 cashew nuts
4 tsp cinnamon powder, freshly ground
4 tbsp fresh mint leaves
6 green cardamom
10 cloves

Method

1. Heat the oil in a large heavy bottomed pan and fry the onions until soft and golden brown.
2. Add the chicken and fry well until browned.
3. Turn the heat down and add the ginger and garlic paste and stir fry well for another 5 minutes.
4. Add the turmeric, salt and garam masala and continue cooking on low heat for 5 minutes.
5. Add 1/2 a cup of boiling water and stir well.
6. Grind all the spices and add them and the ghee to the chicken, stirring well and continue cooking on low heat for 30 minutes.
7. Drain the rice and cook this with 1/2 tsp salt and boiling water in a separate pan. Boil for 12 minutes and drain well when cooked.
8. Layer the rice and the lamb to serve and garnish with sprigs of mint.

Tomato Rice

Ingredients

1 cup basmati rice

2 medium onions, finely sliced

6 ripe tomatoes, pureed

6 green cardamom

1/2 tsp shahzeera

2 x 3" pieces cinnamon

1 tbsp vegetable oil

1 tbsp ghee

1 tsp salt, or to taste

1 1/2 cups hot water

Method

1. Wash and soak the rice in cold water for 20 minutes.
2. Heat the oil and ghee in a pan and turn the heat down.
3. Fry the shahzeera, cinnamon and onions until light brown.
4. Rinse the rice and add it to the pan and fry it for 2 minutes.
5. Steam, skin and puree the tomatoes and add this to the rice.
6. Add the hot water, making sure the liquid from the tomatoes and water is approximately twice the amount of the rice (2 cups worth).
7. Cook on low heat for 10 minutes.
8. Grind the cardamom to make a fine powder and stir in gently into the rice.
9. Continue cooking on low heat for a further 10 minutes, until the rice is cooked.

Lemon Rice

Ingredients

1 cup basmati rice
2 cups water
1 tsp salt, or to taste
Juice of 3 lemons
1 tsp grated root ginger

Ingredients for the garnish

2 tbsp vegetable oil
1 tsp black mustard seed
1 tbsp urad daal
1 tbsp channa daal
1 tbsp peanuts
8-10 curry leaves
2 dry red whole chillies
1 tsp turmeric
1/2 tsp salt, or to taste

Method

1. Rinse and soak the rice in cold water for 20 minutes. Drain, add 2 cups boiling water and salt and cook until *al dente* and drain the excess water. Set aside in a large bowl to cool.

2. Drain the rice and let it cool down.

3. In a separate pan, heat the oil and turn the heat down before adding mustard seeds, urad daal, channa daal, peanuts and curry leaves. Fry these gently for 3-4 minutes until light brown.

4. Add the dry chillies, turmeric and salt and take off the heat and keep the pan covered until slightly cool.

5. Add the juice of 3 lemons and grated ginger to the pan and mix well.

6. Gently add the cooked rice and mix well, but try not to break the rice.

7. Add more lemon juice if you would like a more tangy taste.

Tamarind Rice

Ingredients

1 cup basmati rice
2 cups water
1 tsp salt, or to taste
2 tbsp sesame oil
1 tsp turmeric
6 tbsp tamarind paste or pulp
2 tbsp dry roasted peanuts

Ingredients to grind

1 tsp sesame seed
1 tsp fenugreek seed
2 tsp coriander seed
1 whole dry red chilli

Ingredients for the garnish

1 tbsp vegetable oil
1 tsp black mustard seed
2 tbsp urad daal
2 tbsp channa daal
10-12 curry leaves
2 whole dry red chillies

Method

1. Rinse and soak the rice in cold water for 20 minutes. Drain, add 2 cups boiling water and salt and cook until *al dente* and drain the excess water. Set aside in a large bowl to cool.

2. Grind the sesame seeds and keep aside.

3. In a small pan, dry roast the fenugreek seeds, coriander seeds and one dry chilli for 1 minute on low heat until the aromas are released. Take off the heat and grind into a powder and set aside.

4. In a separate pan, heat the vegetable oil, turn the heat down and add all the ingredients listed under 'For the garnish' for 2 minutes, making sure the chilli does not burn. Take off the heat and set aside.

5. Once the rice has cooled, mix in the turmeric powder, sesame oil, peanuts and tamarind paste into the rice very gently so as not to break the rice.

6. Add the ground spices and the garnish and mix into the rice gently.

7. Put the rice into a serving dish and decorate with the two whole red chillies on top.

The Qutb Shahi Tombs complex of about 30 tombs on raised platforms includes the
last resting places of all seven rulers of the Qutb Shahi dynasty that ruled Golconda
from 1518 to 1687. These domed structures present a blend of Persian and Indian forms,
with pointed arches and intricately carved stonework.

*A strong watercolour wash was applied to the sky and the trees to
allow this building to stand out. The wall shading was modified
to match the lower level of the structure for continuity and the
brickwork was simplified so as not to distract from the dome.*

- Elizabeth Adams

Coconut Rice

Ingredients

1 cup basmati rice
2 cups water
1 tsp salt, or to taste
2 cups freshly grated coconut
2 tbsp fresh coriander 2 tbsp

Ingredients for the garnish

vegetable oil
1 tbsp urad daal
1 tbsp channa daal
1 tsp black mustard seed
10-12 curry leaves
1 whole dry red chilli

Method

1. Rinse and soak the rice in cold water for 20 mins. Drain, add 2 cups boiling water and salt and cook until al dente and drain the excess water. Set aside in a large bowl to cool.

2. In a separate pan, heat the oil and turn the heat down before adding the urad daal, channa daal and mustard seeds and fry for 2 minutes.

3. Add the curry leaves and dry chilli and take off the heat after 30 seconds.

4. Once the rice has cooled, add the grated coconut and freshly chopped coriander, along with the garnish to the rice and mix them in gently so as not to break the rice.

Salad, Raita & Chutney

Golconda Fort began as a mud fort, built about 1143 by the Kakatiya dynasty that ruled most of the eastern Deccan, it was converted into a massive granite structure in the 16th century by the first three rulers of the Qutb Shahi dynasty. Trade in the local Golconda diamonds flourished, with the fort providing a strong vault where they could be held. After falling to Aurangzeb in 1687 the fort fell into ruin, as it remains today.

Although pen and ink was requested, this old fort could not be depicted successfully without relying heavily on a charcoal pencil to recreate the ancient walls and brickwork on the beautiful fort. The brickwork was drawn first and softened with several coats of watercolour paint. Ink was then used to highlight the doors and windows.

- Elizabeth Adams

Kachumbar

Salad

Ingredients

2 medium onions

2 firm tomatoes

1 medium cucumber

1 bunch fresh coriander

2 small green chillies

1/4 tsp salt, or to taste

Juice of 2 limes

Method

1. Dice the onions into tiny pieces and put into a mixing bowl.
2. De-seed the tomatoes and cucumber and dice them into equally small pieces.
3. Cut the fresh coriander finely and add this to the bowl.
4. De-seed (optional for less heat) and cut the chillies using a fork and sharp knife into tiny pieces.
5. Add the salt and mix well.
6. Pour over the juice of two limes and mix well just before serving.

Raita

Spiced Yogurt with Onions, Tomatoes and Cucumber

Ingredients

2 cups natural yogurt
1 medium onion
2 firm tomatoes
1 medium cucumber
1 tsp cumin powder
1/2 tsp salt, or to taste
1/4 cup water

Ingredients for optional garnish

1 tbsp vegetable oil
1 tsp black mustard seeds
6-8 curry leaves

Method

1. Put the yogurt and cold water into a mixing bowl and stir well so that there are no lumps.
2. De-seed the tomatoes and cucumber.
3. Finely dice the tomatoes, cucumber and onion and add it to the yogurt.
4. Add the salt and most of the cumin powder.
5. Mix well and put into a serving bowl.
6. Sprinkle the remaining cumin powder on top before serving.

Method for optional garnish

1. Heat the oil in a small pan.
2. Turn the heat down and add the mustard seed and curry leaves to the oil and fry for 3 minutes, making sure they do not burn.
3. Add this garnish on top just before serving.

Orange Raita

Spiced Yogurt with Orange

Ingredients

2 cups natural yogurt
2 oranges
1/2 tsp cumin powder
1/4 tsp salt, or to taste
1/2 tsp garam masala
1/4 cup water

Ingredients for optional garnish

1 tbsp vegetable oil
1 tsp black mustard seeds
6-8 curry leaves

Method

1. Put the yogurt and cold water into a mixing bowl and stir well so that there are no lumps.
2. Cut the oranges into segments, without the skin or membrane.
3. Add the oranges to the yogurt and mix in gently.
4. Add the cumin powder, salt and most of the garam masala.
5. Pour into a serving bowl and sprinkle the remaining garam masala on top to decorate before serving.

Method for optional garnish

1. Heat the oil in a small pan.
2. Turn the heat down and add the mustard seed and curry leaves to the oil and fry for 3 minutes, making sure they do not burn.
3. Add this garnish on top just before serving.

Cucumber Raita

Spiced Yogurt with Cucumber

Ingredients

2 cups natural yogurt
1 cucumber
1/2 tsp cumin seed
1/4 tsp salt, or to taste
1/8 tsp chilli powder

Method

1. Put the yogurt and cold water into a mixing bowl and stir well so that there are no lumps.
2. De-seed the cucumber and grate it.
3. Add the cucumber to the yogurt and mix in gently.
4. Add the cumin powder and salt and stir well.
5. After putting this into a serving bowl, decorate by sprinkling the chilli powder on top before serving.

Hara Masala Raita

Green Spiced Yogurt

Ingredients

2 cups natural yogurt
2 tbsp fresh coriander
2 tbsp fresh mint leaves
1 green chilli
1/4 tsp salt, or to taste
1/4 cup water

Method

1. Put the yogurt and cold water into a mixing bowl and stir well so that there are no lumps.
2. Wash and blend the coriander, mint and green chilli into a smooth paste, using 2 tbsp of water.
3. Add the fresh herbs and salt to the yogurt and mix making swirls with a metal spoon.
4. Decorate with a sprig of mint.

Mint Chutney

Ingredients

1 large bunch fresh mint leaves

1/2 bunch of fresh coriander leaves

1 medium onion, chopped

2 green chillies

4 cloves garlic

2 tsp tamarind paste

1 tsp salt, or to taste

1/2 cup water

Method

1. Blend all the ingredients in a food processor until you have a smooth paste.
2. This can be stored in an air tight container in the fridge for up to one week.

Tomato Chutney

Ingredients

6 ripe tomatoes
1 medium onion
3 red chillies
1/2 tsp turmeric
1 tsp salt, or to taste
2 tbsp channa daal
2 tbsp vegetable oil
6 tbsp water

Ingredients for the garnish

1 tbsp vegetable oil
6-8 curry leaves
1 whole dry red chilli
1 tsp black mustard seed

Method

1. Wash and chop the tomatoes, onions and chillies.
2. Heat the oil in a pan and add the onions and cook on low heat until soft, but not brown.
3. Add the tomatoes, chillies, turmeric, salt and water and continue cooking.
4. Wash and drain the channa daal and add this to the tomatoes and continue cooking covered and on low heat for 30 minutes.
5. Add a little more water, if necessary, to make a thick sauce.
6. In a separate pan, heat the oil, and turn the heat down before adding the curry leaves and mustard seed.
7. Fry these for 1 min and turn the heat off before adding the whole dry chilli and set aside.
8. Once the tomatoes have cooled down, put the mixture in a blender and whisk it for 30 seconds.
9. Put this into a serving dish and add the garnish on top.

Dessert

The Tank Bund is an earth dam holding back the Hussein Sagar Lake, along the top of which runs a road linking the twin cities of Hyderabad and Secunderabad. The lake was created in 1563 by damming a tributary of the Musi river. Today the road is flanked by 34 statues of local personalities, including rulers, poets, dancers, freedom fighters and social reformers.

This is a close resemblance of this famous road. The watercolour paint is applied heavily on the water and foliage. The palms were created with a very fine art brush.

- Elizabeth Adams

Double ka Meetha

Bread Pudding

Ingredients

10 slices white bread
2 tbsp ghee (clarified butter)
1/2 litre full fat milk
1/2 cup double cream
1/2 cup castor sugar
1/2 cup water

2 tsp rose water
10-12 blanched almonds, sliced or pistachios or both
15 raisins
1 tbsp saffron

Method

1. Pre-heat the oven to 180 °C.
2. Cut the slices of bread slices in half and fry in ghee in a large pan until golden brown on both sides. Set aside and drain excess ghee on kitchen paper.
3. Pour the milk and double cream into a milk pan and boil on a medium heat, stirring well so that it doesn't stick or burn at the bottom of the pan. This will take about 20 minutes until it is condensed to half its quantity.
4. In a separate pan, boil the sugar and water on a medium heat to make the sugar syrup. Stir well until you see little bubbles on the surface. Add the rose water to the syrup and stir well.
5. Use an oven to table dish. Grease it lightly and layer the bread evenly in the dish.
6. Pour the condensed milk and sugar syrup onto the bread, and set aside for 15 minutes so that the bread soaks in the liquids well.
7. Sprinkle the sliced almonds and pistachios, raisins and lightly crushed saffron on top, cover with foil and cook in the oven for 20 minutes.
8. This can be served hot or at room temperature.

Shahi Tukra

Bread Pudding

Ingredients

2 1/2 cups full fat milk
1/2 can sweet condensed milk
1 tsp saffron, slightly crushed
3 tbsp paneer, chopped finely
5 cardamom

6 slices white bread
3 tbsp ghee (clarified butter)
2 tbsp cashew nuts
2 tbsp pistachios
2 tbsp blanched almonds

Method

1. Mix the milk and condensed milk in a pan and stir while boiling on medium heat for 15 minutes, until it is thick and condensed to half its quantity.

2. Add saffron and mix well.

3. Turn the heat off and add the paneer and mix in gently and let the mixture cool down well.

4. Cut the crusts off the bread, cut each slice into two triangles or four square pieces and fry in ghee on low heat until both sides are golden brown. Set aside and drain excess ghee on kitchen paper.

5. Arrange the crisp fried bread neatly in a serving dish and pour the milk mixture on and around the bread.

6. Garnish with the chopped nuts and a few strands of saffron.

7. This can be served hot, at room temperature or put in the fridge and served cold.

Sheer Korma

Dry Vermicelli Pudding

(served at breakfast on Eid Day)

Ingredients

100 gms vermicelli

1 litre full fat milk

1 tbsp ghee (clarified butter)

6 tbsp chopped dates

2 tbsp chopped blanched almonds

2 tbsp pistachios

6 cardamom

Method

1. Heat the ghee in a large frying pan, and fry the vermicelli on low heat for 5 minutes.
2. Warm the milk in a separate pan and add it little by little to the vermicelli, and stir gently until the vermicelli is fully covered.
3. Add the chopped dates and blanched almonds and continue cooking on low heat for a further 10 minutes.
4. Take the seeds out of the cardamom and crush them gently before adding them to the vermicelli.
5. Take off the heat and garnish with slightly crushed pistachios before serving.

Phirni (Firni)

Rice Pudding

Ingredients

1 cup basmati rice
2 1/2 cups full fat milk
5 tbsp castor sugar
10 cardamom

2 tbsp blanched almonds, finely sliced
2 tbsp pistachios, chopped
8-10 strands saffron

Method

1. Wash and soak the rice in cold water for 20 minutes.
2. Drain all the water and cook the rice with the milk on low heat. Stir well all the time to prevent it sticking to the bottom of the pan and getting lumpy. Add a little extra hot milk if required.
3. Take the cardamom seeds out and crush them roughly and add them to the pan, along with the sliced almonds.
4. Continue cooling on low heat, stirring frequently, until the rice is well cooked and a thick consistency is achieved.
5. Turn the heat off and pour into a large serving bowl or individual dessert bowls.
6. Garnish with chopped pistachios and a few saffron strands.
7. This can be served hot, at room temperature or cold from the fridge.

Rose Falooda

Vermicelli Pudding with Rose Syrup

Ingredients

50 gms rice vermicelli

2 cups full fat milk

4 tbsp castor sugar

4 tbsp rose water

2 tbsp rose syrup

6 tsp chia seeds

Strawberry or raspberry jelly

Vanilla ice cream

2 tbsp pistachios

Method

1. Cover and soak the rice vermicelli in boiling water for 10 minutes, until soft. Drain, rinse under cold water, cut into smaller lengths and save for later.

2. Heat the milk in a pan together with the sugar, stirring frequently, until the sugar has dissolved and the milk has thickened a little bit.

3. Add half the rose water to the milk and stir well.

4. Take off the heat, and let it cool down completely before putting it into the fridge until it is cold.

5. Soak the chia seeds in 2 cups of water for 30 minutes. Drain and keep aside.

6. Serve in individual glass bowls or glasses. Put a spoon of chia seeds, followed by a spoon of rose water, jelly, rose flavoured milk, a scoop of vanilla ice cream, vermicelli. Top it with a spoon of rose syrup and chopped pistachio nuts.

Mango Falooda

Vermicelli Pudding with Mango

Ingredients

50 gms rice vermicelli
2 cups full fat milk
4 tbsp castor sugar
4 tbsp rose syrup

6 tbsp chia seeds
6 Alphonso mangoes
Vanilla or mango ice cream

Method

1. Cover and soak the vermicelli in boiling water for 10 minutes, until soft. Drain, rinse under cold water, cut into smaller lengths and save for later.
2. Heat the milk in a pan together with the sugar, stirring frequently, until the sugar has dissolved and the milk has thickened a little bit.
3. Take off the heat, and let it cool down completely before putting it into the fridge until it is cold.
4. Soak the chia seeds in 2 cups of water for 30 minutes. Drain and keep aside.
5. Dice one mango into small pieces and save it for later.
6. Cut and pulp the remaining mangoes in a food processor. Do not add any water, as you want a thick consistency.
7. Serve in individual glass bowls or glasses. Put one spoon of chia seeds, followed by a spoon of mango pulp, one spoon of rose syrup, a little vermicelli, followed by the sweetened milk and one scoop of ice cream. Repeat the same again. Top it with a spoon of rose syrup and a few pieces of diced mango before serving.

Khubani ka Meetha

Apricot Pudding

Ingredients

100 gms dried apricots

100 gms softened apricots

1 cup water

3 tbsp castor sugar

10 blanched almonds

300 ml double cream

Method

1. Cut the apricots into small pieces and discard the stones.
2. Put the apricots and water into a large pan and cook them on high heat till it begins to boil. Stir well, making sure it doesn't stick to the bottom of the pan.
3. Turn the heat down, cover and cook for 30 minutes, stirring occasionally. Add a little more hot water if necessary.
4. The apricots should be well cooked and turn into a pulp consistency. Use a potato masher if necessary, but leave a few bits as well.
5. Add the sugar and stir in well and continue cooking on low heat for a further 5 minutes.
6. Beat the cream so that it is thickened.
7. Cut the blanched almonds in thin strips.
8. Serve in individual bowls and garnish with a dollop of cream and sprinkle of chopped almonds.
9. This can be served hot or at room temperature.

Spices

Set on its own island, this Statue of the Buddha in Hussein Sagar Lake was erected in 1992. Carved in white granite, the statue is 18m tall and a beautiful sight by day or when illuminated at night.

The pen and ink highlighting of the Buddha was chosen for impact rather than realism, as was the heavy coat of paint on the foliage in front of the Buddha. The soft foliage in the background contrasts with the strong leaves in the foreground.

- Elizabeth Adams

Sambhar Powder

Ingredients

10 gms coriander seeds

10 gms fenugreek seeds

10 gms black mustard seeds

10 gms cumin seeds

10 dry curry leaves

2 tsp turmeric powder

2 dry whole red chilli, medium

1 tbsp vegetable oil

Method

1. Heat the vegetable oil in a frying pan.
2. Turn heat down and fry the curry leaves for 1 minute, until crisp. Save these on some kitchen paper.
3. Add the red chilli to the same pan, fry on low heat for 20 second on both sides and save on kitchen paper.
4. Add the coriander, fenugreek, mustard and cumin seeds to the pan and fry on low heat for 1 minute, making sure they do not burn. Save them on kitchen paper.
5. Once all of the above are cool, grind them together into a fine dry powder.
6. You can store the powder in an air tight jar in your larder for future use.

Garam Masala

Ingredients

20 gms shahzeera

20 gms cumin seed

10 gms black peppercorns

10 gms coves

3" piece cinnamon

20 cardamom

3 black cardamom

2 star anise

Method

1. Dry roast all the above ingredients in a frying pan for 30 seconds on low heat.
2. Once completely cool, grind them together into a fine dry powder.
3. You can store this in an air tight jar in your larder for future use.

List of Common Spices

*Spices are usually available at most supermarkets
or Indian grocery stores*

Adrak	Ginger
Chakra Phool	Star anise
Curry Patta	Curry leaves, fresh or dried
Dalchini	Cinnamon
Dhaniya	Coriander
Dhaniya Powder	Coriander powder
Elaichi	Cardamom
Haldi	Turmeric powder
Imli	Tamarind
Kala Namak	Rock salt
Khus Khus	Poppy seed
Lal Mirchi	Red chilli powder
Lehsun	Garlic
Long	Cloves
Methi	Fenugreek seed
Methi Leaves	Fenugreek leaves, fresh or dry
Nimbu	Lemon or Lime
Papaya	Paw Paw
Pudina	Mint
Rai	Black mustard seed
Sabut Lal Mirchi	Whole dry red chilli
Shahzeera	Caraway seeds
Tej Patta	Bay leaves
Til	Sesame seed
Zeera	Cumin

Notes & Useful Tips

Notes

Things you can make and store in an airtight jar for use for up to 8 weeks:

Ginger and garlic paste, in the fridge

Garam masala, in a larder cupboard

Sambhar powder, in a larder cupboard

Useful Tips

The use of a heavy copper-bottomed pan is recommended. This allows even heat while cooking and is particularly good for slow cooking.

Recommend wooden spatulas with a small head or spoon so that the spices can be mixed in well without damaging the main ingredients.

Always heat the oil well, but turn the heat down when frying onions until they are soft and browned. They are likely to burn otherwise.

Always fry onions and spices on a low heat until you see the oil bubbling on the surface. This is a good indication that the spices are cooked.

Wash the pan only once it has cooled down completely.

Most of these recipes can be made a day in advance, but remember to garnish them on the day, after heating through and ready to serve.

Use high quality basmati rice. Rinse and soak the rice for 20 minutes before cooking it.

When cooking steamed rice, add lots of boiling water to cook with, and then drain the excess water just before the rice is tender. Cover with a sheet of kitchen towel and an air tight lid, and leave for 10 minutes before serving. You are guaranteed to have fluffy rice and less starch.

Blanched almonds: Soak whole almonds with their skins on overnight in warm water. It is easy to peel the skin and the almonds are softened and taste better than ready bought blanched almonds.

Index of Recipes

Breakfast

Meat

Fish & Seafood

Eggs, Lentils & Vegetables

Biryani & Rice

Salad, Raita & Chutney

Desserts

Spices

Notes & Useful Tips